I0521894

NAKED

Clare Calvo

blue ocean press
tokyo

Published by:

blue ocean press, an imprint of Aoishima Research Institute
#807-36 Lions Plaza Ebisu
3-25-3 Higashi, Shibuya-ku
Tokyo, Japan 150-0011

Email: books@blueoceanpublications.com
URL: http://www.blueoceanpublications.com

ISBN: 978-4-902837-60-5

Table of Contents

These pages have no organization of thought as I have made a firm attempt to keep my flow as organic and raw as possible. Most of the words tell an experiential tale while others have been inspired by the many elements in life. Each and every expression reveals both love and fear taking form in written word. Some may personally resonate with you while others may not... and such is life through different lenses.

I give thanks to my dharma soul mate on this magical journey of life and beyond. I also give thanks to my friends and family, most especially my mom and dad, who have loved and cared for me unconditionally and supported me in every way. I am grateful to all of God's creation for adding so effortlessly to my inspiration.

Infinite Blessings,
C

GUAMERICA

they say, cleanliness is next to godliness
and so i liver cleansed and colon cleansed
gallbladder cleansed, even got some friends to do
that 21-day detox cleanse
so why do i still try to detoxify
searching with my inner eye
there is a deeper cry for purity
you see, i try to see what part of me
must be set free
am i clean enough
good enough
like you enough
for your salvation
for this nation
to recognize
our people's cries
for equality
you see, overseas
you left your dis-"ease"
with our people, our trees
our oceans... so please
don't take this the wrong way
when i say
it's time to clean up before you build up
your empire of weaponry
set your conscience free
and take responsibility
for that toxic mess

which you continue to invest
i guess
time will tell
what we already know too well
you see, its seeped into our drinking wells
but hey, don't ask, don't tell
right?
i mean, why fight
the red blue & white
when they saved us from plight
with our asian neighbors
you were our supposed "saviors"
saving our lives saving our land
yet now you demand
that same land
land not for sale
land where our ancestors dwell
so, if you fail to take heed
your own hell you'll conceive
cause blood still runs deep
in the soil below concrete
earth knows
trees know
water knows
we know
who is friend and who is foe
SHE does not belong to us
nor we to her
so, all this time

i've come to find
it's been my spirit cryin
to feel pure
pure for me and pure for her
so, cleanse your hands
as i cleanse my soul
i believe that as a whole
we can reach a new goal
to co-exist
in this cosmic bliss
without guns without fists
in the air
clean air
i mean, don't you care
can't we share these things
that we try to own
forgetting that they're only on loan
i still hear her moan
to be treated with respect
and to no longer neglect
HER
our home
GUAM

WE

you say i disappear and that u miss me

i explain i only shape shift so look closely

like the sun in the sky

behind clouds passing by

vision forms new perspectives

and constant changing objectives

so, if you live solely by senses

and buy into pretenses

you'll come to find

that there is no rewind

so, keep it flowing with the river

and be ready to deliver

a rebirth of you

as i birth again too

all along you'll see

there is only "we"

coming all from 1 source

made of the same force

i am always with you

since i am made of you...

HIGHWAY 1

In my oceanic journey
I dive the waves that crash before me
Below the turbulent surface
Where I'm called to glimpse my purpose
As I come up for salty air
In the distance, I feel her stare

She sees my every vision
And feels my every thought
Calling me to dive deep again
Giving back to her what I've caught

A piece of me in naked truth
A mermaid living eternal youth
These sacred pearls of time reveal
What only the mind can conceal
So, hear my song without control
These untamed lyrics come from my soul...

ONE LOVE

Losing faith in the human race
Had me wondering if it was just a waste
Of time
This crime of passion
Seems to be the latest fashion
To try and hold down another
If they got a different accent, sexuality, religion, or color
Have we forgotten the true meaning of life
Cause it sure ain't about winning a race
And if it is
Why would you wanna be first place
If the finish line is basically your life line
Too late There's no rewind
So be kind
No rewind
If I could rewind time
The things I'd do different in this life of mine
But I'm fine
Really I have no regrets
I've learned to forgive
Maybe not completely forget
But who would let life go by
And not at least try
To make a difference
In any instance
You stand for something
Or you fall for anything
Right

Or is that just contributing to the constant fight
Left right
Black White
Gay Straight
Love Hate
Do you see the duality in me
As me
In all
Together we rise and together we fall
Zero degrees of separation
One Love One Light One Nation
Under God
One nation under One God
Yet we've decided
To stay divided
In any and every way we can
Completely ignoring the original plan
Although we are many our source is One
7 billion spinning around the same sun
Our differences are what we need to embrace
Rather than try to erase
Every face
That doesn't agree with our own opinion
Who gave anyone dominion
Anyway
Today is a new day
And we're moving in a new way
That's right
As One

One Light One Love
Within Around Above

Late start to an early end

Frozen kisses in time

Only reveal what was left behind

In this linear illusion

Created to organize our confusion

Grasping with both hands

Our individual plans

Holding each breath

As we cling to our nest

Hold tight and breathe light

As we lose the fight

Against our own mind

We come to find

The struggle is 'not accepting'

Pushing rather than letting

Let go

Trust the flow~ And know...

LOVE (1)

I see Him in my mind's eye
I hear him between each cry
Of sorrow and of pain
Because it really is all the same
These tears I cry
Uncover each lie
I've seen and heard
Thought deed and word
Saltwater from these eyes
Help me to recognize
That I am the prize
I have been seeking to win
Searching everywhere but within
Liquid sorrow down my face
I've learned to embrace
Each story told
That my mind would unfold
Surrendering to all
On my knees I fall
Face to Earth I Bow
In this eternal now.

LOVE (2)

What is beauty if not to be expressed?
What is a love song without the soul undressed?
Uninhibited passion never will allow
the dance of life to end its Waltz without a final bow.
An unexpected season has come and gone this time.
Though only for a moment, the moment was sublime.
Unforgettable visions throughout a silent night;
indescribable sensation through crashing waves and
moonlight.
There is no gift more precious than inspiration from
another.
I take this gift and fly away with new treasures to
discover.

LOVE (3)

I lay here awake unable to sleep
Wanting your body next to mine
The warmth of your arms the touch of your lips
drunken me like the sweetest fine wine
Though you're not in this space nor in this time
Forever you remain in the depths of my mind.

LOVE (4)

Don't change the mood voluptuous moon
Don't let the sun come out too soon
Every inch of my flesh needs to be exposed
Exposed to moonlight Exposed to twilight
While my body begins to excite
My soul takes off to flight
Uninhibited body stands alone at the window
As light from the moon casts a shadow
Another silhouette joins the single body
But instead of two, the figures move as one
Slowly descending on to the floor
As unspoken words cry out for more
Flesh on flesh
Deepens the breath
Gripping tight
All throughout the night
Cold marble floor turns hot with passion
As bodies move without exasperation
Lip to lip, hip to hip
Palms on thighs, increasing grip
Intertwine we begin to unwind
Unwind the mind as we combine
Hypnotic beat, the force goes deep
Flesh on flesh, with rhythmic breath
Cannot depart, creating art
Art in motion, ecstatic notion
Bodies united, becoming excited

Exchanging sweat, becoming wet.

FEAR (1)

As traffic goes by and summer turns to fall
Here I dance in my sleep
As stocks take a dive and Saturn starts to rise
Here I dance in my sleep
The song is unfamiliar yet the words ring true
My body remembers all that my mind does not let
through
My dance with love comes and goes as I please
While asleep through the night I move with ease
Trust in love embraces me at night
But when awake fear holds on too tight
Afraid to take the hand of love and dance all night and
day
Afraid to let the music move me while the tears sweep
fear away.

LOVE (5)

I felt Him inside me deep and warm
His presence devoured me whole without harm
The core of my fruit lay bitter yet sweet
As he tasted each drop of my vaporized heat
Candle burns mark each drop of delight
Feathers of passion rose his sword to new heights
The hours escaped us as night gave to day
Moment by moment blessing life a new way.

FEAR (2)

Extra! Extra! Read all about it!
Let's blow them outta their holes.
Let's stand united and conquer our goals.
Let's find the predator and kill, kill, kill.
Let's beat 'em down till they bow down and kneel.
We are the way, we chant, sing, and pray
Retaliate against us and you will definitely pay.
Do you really think we want to help our allies
And that's where tax dollars go?
If you ain't got nothing to offer
You might as well be our foe.
Some nations receive no aid while others do?
Does it really have a thing to do with Muslim, Christian,
or Jew?
Power of Love over Love of Power
Let the truth set us free on this 7th Hour.

DANCE

my senses all five senses alive and in constant wonder as
the beat of the drums filled my body with jolts of
emotion my mind stood still in utter devotion to my
sense of sound all around my sight took interest in
circular motion the hue of each persons' complexion
beautiful rainbow of light to dark and dark to light all
blending together into the night then drum gave to
dance and dance on to drum i felt my body become one
with the One vibrations ran through the tips of each
finger down my back & to my legs flowing like a river
lost in my trance as raindrops kissed my salty lips open
my eyes to the sweetest solar eclipse.

LOVE (6)

when the sun kisses my cheek in the cold of december
when a breeze in july sends me hints of coriander
these are the moments i feel GOD
when voices in harmony seduce tears from eyes
or the djembe drum beckons my spirit to rise
these are the moments i feel GOD
when a baby exposes her first tooth with a smile
or a lady about 80 shares stories of her life for a while
these are the moments i feel GOD... Gifts Of Divinity
between ALL
within ALL
as ALL

LOVE (7)

This is but a dream to live with untainted desires of love
To reach far into the waves of energy above and beyond
this time and space
I occupy
Tears of joy I cry
Awaiting my golden day in the sun
Yet content in knowing I praise none
Other than the Divine, the One, the Love, what we're
made of.

LOVE (8)

Incense burning to the tip with you and me and he and she melted into it Each owns throne Again and then you touch the lining of my own Light upon the oceans reflected night Gracing my sight to the darkness below Embracing the land called Guam Reminding us who we are and where we're from.

LOVE (9)

Pleasure my uncertainty
As I allow these thoughts to free
Interject my Being
As images create new feeling
Create in me
A sea of curiosity
A constant thirst for more
To explore
So much to choose
With no thing to lose
For nothing is lost or can be found
What goes up must come down
Laws of the Universe
Satisfy this thirst at first
Then I discover more in store
I've yet to explore
Hence the cycles and circles of time
Continue to flow in a constant rhyme
No where to get to yet somewhere to go
With ease and grace we become the flow...

YEMAYA

Laughter filled the air as the ship set off to sea
Young lives of innocence awaited what came to be
The tides took height like none before
Fear grew deep as they faded from shore
Thunderous waves shook all hope at last
As prayers were shouted the horror came to past
Mystery remains as to what spared those lives
Except those who know Sea answers when she hears the
cries

LOVE (10)

I want to fly to where the Earth meets the sky
I want to skydive into a mornings sunrise
Through the clouds and to the universe
I search my course
Through time and space
Let me walk this place
With every reason to smile
For in a long or short while
My time will be through
And once again I'll come home to YOU

FEAR (3)

The future unknown shivers fear to the bone
As I dance with my soul playing my role
A slave unsold yet here to hold
Hand in hand we dance with the land
Where he is me and I am you
Owning and selling our souls untrue
Fear of the other no sister nor brother
To claim as one's own through the madness we roam
Searching for love below and above
With eyes full of fear
Illusions of love disappear
With a heart full of love
We're reminded it's what we're of.
Nothing to get and nothing to give
All things to do and all reasons to live.

LOVE (11)

Alone I came and alone I'll leave
And all the while I still believe
There are those souls along the way
That pour more beauty into each new day
For so long I have searched to find
A happiness outside of mine
My mind in time I will come to find
Need not search far for such love sublime
My heart so true revealed to you
Creates this force of life anew
Birthed not from you nor from me
This force vibrates new energy
My stride has changed
Through new eyes I'm seeing
Our experience has altered
The core of my Being
So alone I came and alone I'll leave
But the essence of you I will forever conceive.

LOVE (12)

This is but a dream to live
with untainted desires of love
To reach far into the waves
of energy beyond and above
This time and space I occupy
Tears of joy I cry
Awaiting my golden day in the sun
Yet content within one
of many ways I praise
None other than the Divine
the Love, the Source
Whatever name of choice.

LOVE (13)

No more tears
Release all fears
To you Beloved
I take your hand
As I walk through sand
With you Beloved
Footprints on my heart
Of your existence
You beat every pulse
In each instance
You feel me whole
As you fill my soul
My Beloved

LOVE (14)

I met a man named Theo who brought me many gifts.
He shared such beauty with me and stole my heart with
just one kiss.
Time took lead without us and truth maintained her
peace.
My heart not healed from past times reflected Theo's
grief.
I witnessed eyes of sadness and had no words to speak.
Blinded by illusions my own grief sunk too deep.
Now I stare within me and relinquish all control
The pattern has been shifted as I release sweet Theo's
soul.

LOVE (15)

Going home to memories of another time
If there were such a thing as a linear time line
Separating day sky and night sky
On these wings I fly
To truths of a new day
Seems so far away
I hear the calls reaffirming my arrival
Yet whispering doubts confirm my denial
I take to these lips a pure kiss for now
I take to this heart no greater love than thou.

LOVE (16)

Turn your words into Song.
Turn your walk into Dance.
And through it all remember
Nothing is by chance.

FEAR (4)

Frozen kisses in time
Only reveal what was left behind
In this linear illusion
Created to organize our confusion
Grasping with both hands
Our individual plans
Holding each breath
As we cling to our nest
Hold tight and breathe light
As we lose the fight
Against our own mind
We come to find
The struggle is 'not accepting'
Pushing rather than letting
Let go
Trust the flow~ And know...

LOVE (17)

She came in Summer
Under a smiling Moon
She held my hand and sang a tune
Of hidden magic
In the deep blue sea
Of an island's treasure
In the roots of each tree
Tales of a People
From times before
Whose dreams were washed upon the shore
They danced in sevens
And sang to the heavens
Invisible to Eyes
They floated the skies
Please take my hand
Lead me back to this land
I pleaded with love
As he flew above
There is only now
She said to me
They are always here
If you could only see
Not with eyes
But with your heart so wise
Blurred vision came clear
As I took one last look
Salt water splashed on me
As the proa shook

She came in summer
Under a smiling Moon
She came and left
me way too soon.

LOVE (18)

Without words, I hear you
Without touch, I feel you
Without thought, I know you
Without effort, I love you

LOVE (19)
These are the times
These are the days
I look around
I walk this ground
All in thanks and praise
You've let me fly so free
You've loved me unconditionally
And accepted me for me
You've let me spread my wings and fly
Knowing there is no real goodbye
Whether together or apart
You are always in my heart

LOVE (20)

I sit and watch the buzzing bees
I sit and watch the dancing trees
Pachamama all around
Clouds in sky to dirt on ground
All made of same ingredients
All are gifts that heaven sent

KRISHNA JANMASHTAMI

Utmost beauty this day unfolds
As we celebrate the birth of Divine
Bow to the alter with sweets at hand
Ecstatic from melodic wine
We sing without words and dance without feet
With the sound of our breath and the drumming hearts
beat.

LOVE (21)

Kind thoughts
Kind words
Kind deeds
Heart bleeds
For others we meet
Yet ourselves we defeat
Over and over
We stomp on our heart
Wondering when
The loving will start
To overflow from another
Forgetting we are our #1 lover

NAKED

When I feel lost, I take off shoes and feel the Earth; I take off clothes and feel the Ocean; I take off ego and feel YOU in me, as me, in all, as all.... my Beloved!

THE TIMES
I try disguise
These tears in my eyes
As I look to the skies
I hear the cries
And I come to realize
That I bought into lies
That were sold
And were told
In Vain
With no shame
In God's name
Yet there's no blame
Nor hate in my heart
This is a new start
That will depart
The past
At last
It's our time
To shine

HEAL

What is it to heal but to come back to our true state of love... all else dissipates & we are as we once were... perfect whole and complete. Can healing really be as simple as that? Love unencumbered? If so, then forgiveness would be the most potent of medicines.

101 INSPIRATIONS

I look all around me and see
that there is enough
there's enough for me
and there is enough for you
Enough for every Christian Muslim Jew
Every Buddhist and all others too
So, there's no need to hoard all resources
or claim to be the chosen forces
No need to continue this fight
in trying to prove who's right
cause it really don't matter, black or white
brown yellow blue or red
"The kingdom of Heaven is Yours"... He said
She said It said
So long as you keep your soul fed
by Him through Him from Him
or Her or It
You see God is not something I can easily fit
into a name label dogma or box
But wait, before you stone me with your rocks
take the pebble out of your own eye
and ask yourself why
why we allow these systems of belief
to cause each other more pain and grief
When the golden rule
The commandment in just about every sacred scripture
is to love one another, just love
your neighbor your brother your sister

Now you may laugh at my idealistic ideology
or consider this possibly bordering blasphemy
and that's alright you see
I love and bless you even so
cause the more life I live the more I've learned to let go
What you think of me is none of my business
I know we are of the same ISness and from that same Oneness
You don't need to agree or even understand me
Just try and make the attempt to see
see through Mother Theresa's eyes
when she said...
"Each one of them is Jesus in disguise"

MY SON

I will show you, my son
Of your worth
Not your value
There is no price tag on dignity and integrity
No capitation on character
You will be lured by valuable exteriors
And question your worthy interiors
Do not confuse the two
The flash of the world will fade
Your inner treasure will sustain you
Mind your belongings and your body

www.ingramcontent.com/pod-product-compliance
Lightning Source LLC
Chambersburg PA
CBHW021005150626
46549CB00012BA/1291